Master The Job Interview

*Proven Tips And Techniques
To Acing The Job Interview*

Table of Contents

Introduction 1

8 Realities of Job Searching 4

The Correct Mindset For Your Job Search and Interview 8

Tips in Preparing for a Phone Interview 10

How an Interviewer Judges the Applicant 13

Step 1: Do Some Research About The Company 16

Step 2: Review Your Online Reputation 21

Step 3: Prepare For Possible Interview Questions And Answers 27

Step 4: Know The Dress Code 34

Waiting For The Interview 37

Step 5: Be Punctual 37

What To Do 38

STEP 6: Be Courteous 41

After The Interview 60

Step 7: Follow Up 60

Most Common Causes of Rejection 62

Several Days Afterwards 66

Step 8: Forward A More Formal Thank You Note 66

Step 9: Wait And Then Follow Up With A Single
Phone Call Or Email 67
What Not To Do After The Interview 69
Conclusion 71

Introduction

I want to thank you and congratulate you for downloading the book, *"Master The Job Interview - Proven Tips And Techniques To Acing The Job Interview"*.

This book contains proven steps and strategies on how to ace an interview.

After designing a winning CV, writing a convincing cover letter and landing an interview with the hiring manager, the final step is acing the interview to complete your job seeking process. In most cases, failing to dedicate some time to prepare for the interview is what often lands people back in the job searching stage rather than the cozy new office chair of their desired company. In fact, studies have showed that up to a third of employers give interview blunders as the most common reason for turning down job applicants. While a trusted relative or friend can be a great source of information in terms of interview advice, when it comes to this information age, certain rules also apply. The key is familiarizing yourself with both the new and old rules of interviewing to ensure you ace that interview. However, once you get that interview right, you have beaten all the other candidates and earned a spot at your new company as the next brilliant employee. You will find yourself working again and earning an income. Given, interviews are not your everyday cup of tea, in order to ace that interview, it takes preparation, practice and acquiring information regarding the needed skills and techniques to impress your potential employers.

This book is just what you need to ace that interview. You will learn important tips, techniques and adequate information to help you land your dream job. Acing an interview has never been easier thanks to this book.

This document is geared towards providing exact and reliable information in regards to the topic and issue covered. The publication is sold with the idea that the publisher is not required to render accounting, officially permitted, or otherwise, qualified services. If advice is necessary, legal or professional, a practiced individual in the profession should be ordered.

- From a Declaration of Principles which was accepted and approved equally by a Committee of the American Bar Association and a Committee of Publishers and Associations.

In no way is it legal to reproduce, duplicate, or transmit any part of this document in either electronic means or in printed format. Recording of this publication is strictly prohibited and any storage of this document is not allowed unless with written permission from the publisher. All rights reserved.

The information provided herein is stated to be truthful and consistent, in that any liability, in terms of inattention or otherwise, by any usage or abuse of any policies, processes, or directions contained within is the solitary and utter responsibility of the recipient reader. Under no circumstances will any legal responsibility or blame be held against the publisher for any reparation, damages, or monetary loss due to the information herein, either directly or indirectly.

Respective authors own all copyrights not held by the publisher.

The information herein is offered for informational purposes solely, and is universal as so. The presentation of the information is without contract or any type of guarantee assurance.

The trademarks that are used are without any consent, and the publication of the trademark is without permission or backing by the trademark owner. All trademarks and brands within this book are for clarifying purposes only and are the owned by the owners themselves, not affiliated with this document.

8 Realities of Job Searching

For those of you who are wondering what's the big deal about job interviews, this section will answer your doubts. Most applicants take job interviews for granted because they are confident with the credentials.

The following are some of the most believed myths in job searching and under them are the realities. It is important to appreciate them because it will motivate you more to do great in your interview.

#1 - College will guarantee a job for me

Having a degree does not guarantee that you will have a job. Sure, being able to finish a 4 year course can give you an advantage because of the knowledge you have gained, but mere knowledge won't get you far. Did you know that companies now think that military personnel are appealing for certain positions since they can benefit from their discipline and hardworking attitude?

The recruiter has to know that there's more to you than just your diploma. And one of the best ways of showing them your skills is by facing them confidently during an interview.

#2 - When I shotgun my resume, I'm sure to have a job!

When you shotgun your resume, it means that you send out as many as you can to a lot of companies that are hiring. This is just a myth. Just because employers received your CV, it does not mean that they won't go straight to the shredder.

The technique is to find the job that is right for you, prepare an outstanding resume, submit it and do well in the scheduled interview. And if you will think about it, sending out a lot of resumes is not practical. The effort and the money will be wasted.

#3 - There's no difficulty in finding a job; you just need to KNOW HOW to find it!

Now, here's another reality check. Just because you know how to find the right job, doesn't mean you will be accepted. Of course, you must have the skills that they require. So be mindful of your assets – as much as possible, attend trainings, seminars, and read a lot about your industry.

You have to understand that even if you get accepted to a job, it does not mean that you will stay there. You have to guard it by making sure you have the right set of skills.

#4 - They'll accept me once I lower my salary expectation.

Most applicants think that their salary expectation plays a huge role in the hiring process. What you have to understand is this: companies already have a specified salary for you, if they think you will become a great asset to the company, they will even increase that range just so you would sign the contract. So, it's not all about the money.

That's not to say though that you should heighten up your expected salary, just research about the average earnings in your industry and stick to that. If you want them to offer you with higher rates, you have to make yourself desirable in their eyes.

#5 - I'll have the best job because I'm qualified

This is supposed to be true, but sadly, it isn't. Some of the best qualified individuals do not get noticed because they do not ace their interviews, or may be because they don't make their resumes outstanding.

So do not be complacent just because you have what it takes to stay in the job– you are not yet hired. Make sure that you ace the application process first, and that includes that interview.

#6 - The recruiters have my best interest

Not to say that all recruiters are ill-natured, but let us be honest. Recruiters are hired to screen applicants for the company. The one signing their paychecks are the administrators of the corporation. They are bound to hire those whom they think will improve their standing as the company's recruiter. So be at your best during the application process, even when the hiring manager is all smiles to you.

#7 - There is no need to sell myself to employers

This is another myth that should be cleared. In job searching, marketing yourself is very important. Think this way: you are the product that can provide them with what they need, but the fact is this: there are also many products that can do the same (A.K.A. applicants). What you need to do is make the company believe that you are the best product out there and that cannot afford to lose.

How can you do that? Of course, by being marketable in the interview process.

#8 - Being over 50 will make it hard to find a job

It's just another myth. Companies now are appreciating the experience of those who are seasoned in the industry. People who are over 50 but have the right set of skills are more likely to get hired than women who are in the stage to have babies. It's because they want their employees to be as productive as possible.

The Correct Mindset For Your Job Search and Interview

1. Your persistence is the key

In business, success cannot be achieved overnight. You cannot give it your all on the first day, get complacent on the second, and then expect return of investment in the third. The same rule applies to job hunting.

It won't just take you one act, there should be several. For example, CV should be passed at least once every two months, depending on the company's policy. If you know a person in the corporation, you might want him to vouch for you– not that you'll use connection to go straight to the hired folder, but to at least let the company know that you are a good person to have in the organization.

2. The interview is a two-way process

Yes, it is a given to let the recruiter lead the process, but you should also interview him or her. That's only natural (you are going to be in the company after all, if you pass) and the hiring manager will not feel offended. Just imagine, if you just let him ask you questions and you contribute nothing to the conversation, it will seem like you just want to get over with.

So, ask for some information, just make sure that what you will ask is not a matter of public record.

3. Be in the company, even when you're still in the application process

Before attending the interview, make a list of the things that you can do, opposite each item, mark down those that are "needed" by the company. Read about them and memorize them. If the company has other requirements that you cannot provide them with, start reading and learning about them.

When the recruiting manager asks you "What can you contribute to the company?" you will know your answers by heart. And if the topic strays on the things that you are still not trained to do, at least you'll have the basic knowledge.

4. Your references matter

When you submit a resume, make sure that you have the right people as your references. Gauge them according to the position you are applying for. And do not forget to warn them— as much as possible, before submitting your CV, they already know that their names were written as reference people. If you have forgotten to tell them, make a call as soon as you have submitted your papers.

Make sure that the people you will choose are in good terms with you.

5. Practice, practice, practice!

Although you really cannot expect anything from the interview, there's nothing wrong with practicing. You can do this alone— face the mirror and rehearse answering the most expected questions they will ask. Watch yourself: from your posture to your expression.

If you have someone with you, ask them to play the role of the recruiting manager. And let them lead the interview too!

Tips in Preparing for a Phone Interview

Most interviews require having a phone interview first before going for the face to face stage. And why not? That is a very practical system. For one, the interviewer will know RIGHT AWAY if the applicant a good fit. The tone of the voice during a phone conversation will already dictate a person's confidence level. If the recruiter deemed the applicant to be lacking, then the chances of a call back is low.

Here are some guidelines on how to ace the phone interview:

1. Think of it as a personal interview

Remember this: most companies will do several sets of interviews—meaning, whether you pass the phone interview or not, you will still be attending the other scheduled face to face interviews. That's very good because in case you mess up on the phone, you will still have the chance to redeem yourself in the personal job interview.

The problem is when the company you are applying to wants a step by step process. It means you have to pass a certain test first, before you will have to chance to move on to the next set of screening. So, if ever you fail the phone interview, that's the end of the road for you— at least in that company.

That is why it is important to treat the phone interview as if it is a personal one.

2. The location

Phone interviews are not surprise. The recruiting manager will politely ask you if "it is a good time to do the interview or if you wish to prepare some more." If you are at an awkward place where it is noise and you become distracted, calmly say so and give the time when it is convenient for you.

Afterwards, choose a location that is quiet, your room is a perfect place because you are comfortable there. Remind your family not to be noisy and not to disturb you during the time of the interview.

3. What you are wearing matters

This is one of the advantages of phone interview— you can wear whatever you want to wear for as long as it is comfortable for you. Wear something that makes you feel good, be it your PJs or a corporate attire. If you feel good, then it will show in the tone of your voice.

4. Avoid having an idiot board

Common mistake made by applicants during a phone interview is this: laying out all their notes in front of them. Don't do that. It will only confuse you— instead on concentrating on getting the questions answered, you will focus on finding your notes!

So keep your answers simple and to the point.

5. Never reveal your salary expectation

It is not advised to reveal the salary expectation during the phone interview. When the recruiter asks you about your expected salary, it is just a ploy to put you on the spot. When asked about it, answer calmly that if everything goes well in the personal interview, then the salary doesn't matter. If he keeps on pressing on, be firm and decline. Tell him that you are not comfortable in giving numbers when you are still not seeing the environment of the company, and how the employees work there.

How an Interviewer Judges the Applicant

In this section you will learn how a recruiter "usually" judges an applicant. That said, you must acknowledge that the following criteria are not true for all companies. They are just being provided to you so that you will know where to concentrate more in case you only have a short time to prepare.

Your past experiences

Although the recruiter already has an insight as to where you previously worked, for how long, and what you position was, he still doesn't know the job description. Prepare this information with care and be detailed. Make sure that you will highlight those responsibilities that are also needed by the company.

If you are a leader or a follower

You might not notice it, but recruiters are also gauging your capability to lead and to follow. Don't lean towards being too much of a leader, you might come off as someone who is subversive. But don't be too much of a follower; they will think you are weak. Yes, the interviewers are looking for balance. Not too strong that you might cause trouble, and not too weak that you won't accomplish anything.

However, it still depends. If the position you are applying for requires for you to become a leader, then be assertive, but remember, not too much.

Honesty

Some interviewers are tricky. They will push you to a point where you will feel like your skills are being doubted. Before you know it, you are nodding your head to the things that you really are not trained to do. Be careful, as we have discussed on the early chapters, interviewers have the ability to see through your lies. So stick to the truth and never give in to their traps.

This also includes instances where you were found out. Honesty should happen in all the process– from the submission of CV to the interview. If they find out inaccuracies in your credentials, they might even file a case for falsification of documents! So always be honest!

Communication

This includes how you carry yourself all throughout the interview process, from your choice of words to the tone, from your body language to your eye contact. Even your handshake is being judged, so don't be too complacent even when the recruiter "asks" you to feel comfortable.

Technical skills

You cannot do much if you really are not techie, but here's the drill: you have to let the employer know that you are willing AND capable of learning. As much as possible explain to them the closest skills you have to the ones they require.

Spontaneity

Your confidence at yourself can make or break your future career. Some interviewers are lazy– they do not want to consume 15-20 minutes in the room trying to figure you out. Their best criterion is if you believe in yourself, and ***it will show*** in your posture, your words, and smile.

The moment you enter the room, convince the interviewer that the job is already yours and the interview is just for formality purposes. Be both natural and professional.

Step 1: Do Some Research About The Company

It has always been preached by career experts that you should research on the company before going to that job interview. Getting adequate information about the company can provide useful insight that might come in handy when answering some of the questions you might be asked during the interview. But what does that mean? For starters, the best places to start are your computer and internet connection, and then tap your network to find all the information and insight that will improve your answers during the interview. So, what should you know?

The Mission Of The Company

If the company you are applying for employment is relatively large, chances are that it already has a website. You can take advantage of this to see the outlook of the company as it wants to appear. While you are at it, take this time to look for the mission statement of the company, and then determine how the position you are applying for relates to this mission. Determine how your background and experience have equipped you to support the perceived goals of the company.

Recent Achievements Of The Company

Most companies usually have a section on their website like a news page or press room page that shows recent news releases. If not, you can always search for news about the company on the internet. You can then relate the news with its long term implications, both for you and the company when you get the job, and then prepare some questions revolving around the news, if it is sensible. Engaging in a well informed conversation with potential employers can be critical in the success of your interview.

Your Interviewers

If there is a search tool on the company's website, use it to look for the names of the people that will be interviewing you. You may find press releases or bio pages that give you insight into their most transparent activities. You can then look for them on LinkedIn or conduct a general web search to find some in-depth information about them. The search might yield some common ground you can bring up in your conversation, for example, a recent professional accomplishment for which you can pay a compliment.

The Industry

The internet can also be a great source of information where you can find out what other people are saying about the company. These include blogs, trade publications and general interest publications as a whole. Search for news about major corporations on national publications. Hometown newspapers can be a convenient source of information on local industries and small businesses. Depending on your field, be prepared to discuss financial prospects on your industry or any other industry trends.

People on the inside

Another great source of information could be the people already employed at the company. These can provide the much needed insight into the corporate culture, business initiatives and probably personality dynamics. Look at your LinkedIn profile to see if you have any connections. In addition, connect with professional organizations and alumni organizations but don't stop there. Ask your friends and relatives if they have someone in the company that might provide some relevant information about your prospective employer.

The Company Compared to Others

A company often has a lot of competitors, especially if the products and services they offer are deeply needed or wanted by consumers. Inevitably, the company you are applying to is not the "only one" in the industry. Why is there a need for you to know the things that set the company apart from the others? For one, it can be a good starting point of a conversation, and it can also give you the "ready feel" if ever your interviewer decides to ask you, "What made you choose our company?"

The fact that you know the company's edge is a testament on how much you really want to become a part of it. So do a little research as to how they are different.

How the public sees the company

If the company you are applying to is huge (meaning they are employing a lot of people), surely, they are capable of circulating news to the media. As someone who wants to become a part of the corporation, you must know how the public reacts about that news. If ever the company is still growing, it does not mean that there are no current affairs. Consider visiting their Facebook page to get the pulse, and see how the people (both working there and using their products or services) are talking about the events in the company.

Examples of things to look for:

- Is there a new product or service?
- Did they launch an improved system of the services they offered?
- What do the people think of these latest feats?
- If there is a room for improvement, what is it according to the public?

Company Structure and Culture

This is pretty simple, just research about the organizational structure of the company, from top authorities to the bottom. Learn about the twists and turns when it comes to application and promotion. Knowing this will make you seem eager to the eyes of the interviewers.

While you are on it, you can also read about the environment "inside" the company. As much as possible, make things realistic– you can point out semi-bad things as long as those are not detrimental to the corporation.

This part is very important; the interviewers will look at you badly if you don't have any idea about the atmosphere of the offices. Why? It's because when you are a future employee, you surely would like to know "how it is" to be there, so you are expected to research or at least ask.

The Future of the Company

And lastly, don't forget to read something about the company's future plans. Being equipped with this knowledge will let the company authorities know that "you want to be there" when those plans are brought to fruition.

Where to do your research?

The best way to get news and knowledge about the company is through their website and social networking accounts. Those are often updated. But don't forget to ask people who already work in the company. So visit forums and post interesting questions and wait for someone to answer your queries.

Step 2: Review Your Online Reputation

Today, more and more companies are embracing the internet and using it as a valuable tool to evaluate prospective employees. In most cases, an online reputation can make or break your success in acing that important job interview. If you want to make a great impression, you need to review your digital footprint (everything associated with your name on the internet). Don't be fooled. Recruiters and companies check search engine results routinely to learn more about their applicants. As such, it is advisable to think about your online persona just as much as your interview attire. Social media red flags and questionable content can take you out of the rat race, but a confident job seeker can incline a positive digital presence. Fortunately, you can screen and safeguard your online reputation to avoid a possible rejection using the following steps:

Find out what others are seeing about you

Search for your name on social media sites and major search engines. If most of the results linked to your name are non-professional, you may want to update your professional profile. You should have at least one of the top results matching your name to your professional interests. One great way to do this is to focus on updating your LinkedIn profile as this has the highest visibility in Google search results.

Put your best foot forward

Your social media profiles can be a great way to showcase your strengths and demonstrate that you are the best person for the job. You can use these social media profiles to illuminate your unique hobbies outside your work life. Post accomplishments freely such as charity work or marathon running. If a potential employer runs into your personal profiles, these unique interests can serve to complement your professional credentials. Quora is a great platform to demonstrate how much knowledge you have as well as your general interests.

Limit negative content

Privacy settings are constantly changing on social sites such as Facebook, and as such, you need to be on the lookout on what you share online to avoid being sorry. After you have reviewed your social site profiles and ascertained that all the content consist of information you wish to share with your potential employers, it is time to scan the remains. Secure. Me for Facebook is a free tool that allows you to review your content, protects your profile from viruses and dangerous links, and keeps track of your friends' posts and photos. Do not post anything you are in doubt of if you think that it may jeopardize your job application in the future.

Make sure there is no confusion

If you share your name with several other people, chances are you might be mistaken for someone else on the internet. To avoid this, find a way to distinguish yourself from everyone else that shares your name. There are several ways you can do this such as including an initial or middle name or incorporating your professional specialty into your name. For example, if your name is Richard Johnson and you are a CPA, you could use "Richard Johnson, CPA" in your online profiles.

A Guide for Personal Branding

Branding is a common strategy for companies because they want people to see them as the best brand for the industry that they are focusing on.

What is personal branding?

Branding is when you are known for a certain quality. For example, a family often goes to a certain restaurant. While the whole family enjoys the menu, the kids only love the dessert. When some people mention that restaurant, the kids will only know the restaurant for desserts.

In that situation, the restaurant is branded for desserts, at least for the kids.

Personal branding is just the same, only now, you are marketing yourself not to the consumers, but to the employers. Your brand can be anything, but when looking for employment, it should be your skills.

How can you brand yourself?

The surefire way of branding yourself is by building the reputation. It will take you a lot of time to brand yourself, but there is a quick fix available.

The quick fix is done by building an online presence. In the following section, you will know how to "build" yourself in the internet.

Step by Step Guide on How to Build Your Online Reputation

A lot of people are now deeply rooted in the internet, not only does the social media serve the purpose of entertainment; they are also used by the employers to "judge" certain candidates. In this light, it is important that your online reputation is unblemished, or what others call a clean slate.

If you think that this idea is ridiculous (how can employers have the time to use Google?!) think again. Did you know that daily, name searches in Google reaches over a billion? And that 77% of those searches are screening from companies? In fact, most recruiters are "required" to search your name as a pre-screening procedure.

In this section you will learn about the step by step guide on building your online reputation– from building certain aspects, to burying things that may ruin you for the company.

#1 - Google your name

The first step involves gaining the baseline data. How do you do that? It's easy. Simply search your name on Google. But before typing your name on the Google search bar, make sure that you have signed out of your Google account. Google has a technique where in it "alters" the search results by basing it on your profile– like location and interests. Since the recruiters won't have that advantage, sign out before doing the search.

Lastly, take note of the name you are using. If in your line of career you often use your second name, and it is what's reflected on your business cards and resume, then use it.

Note: Don't forget that Google is not the sole search engine; also search your name using others like Bing, Yahoo, and MSN.

#2 - Analyses of Results

Yes, you should also perform it. In this section you will know whether your reputation is bad or good. Consider the following categories of reputation:

Negative Reputation - This is the category you want to avoid because it can literally break your opportunity in a second. And no, it does not have to be a severe case (like when politicians are accused of corruption), just a simple status update, a blog post about you, a photo or worse, a video depicting you in a very bad manner can have the recruiters shaking their heads.

Example: A photo or a video where you were seen to be having a scandalous fight with anyone. Recruiters do not want violence in their company so why would they choose you if you seem to be volatile?

Insignificant Reputation - This category neither helps nor ruins you. It can be for various reasons. For an instance your online standing is outdated. You haven't had any news for years! Or may be the posts, photos, and statuses are all about you but it does not have anything to do with your career. The recruiters will only feel frustrated when this results show up.

Example: You have a blog dedicated to your favorite TV series. Now think about it, what will the recruiters do with that information? Nothing.

Positive Reputation - This is your goal category. When recruiters classify your rep as positive, the chances of them hiring you are higher. This means that when they searched your name on Google, they saw an update on your career.

Examples: Gaining an award, attending a seminars and having a blog dedicated to your progressing experience are good examples.

#3 - Improving your reputation

Now that you know where you stand, you must be able to improve it, especially if you're on the negative and irrelevant category.

When I don't have an online presence - You have to start now. In fact, this is much better than having a lot of negative presence. Get a pen and paper and list down all the things you want your employers to know about you. Facebook is a good starting point, so post photos that show your good sides in your career. There is also LinkedIn. When using that website, make sure that you share "relevant" articles involving your profession.

When I want to build certain information - If you already have a website dedicated to your profession, and you just want to build it so that companies can easily see it, you must learn how to "optimize" the site. That means you'll use certain keywords that are appealing to Google. This process will take some time, and if you have zero knowledge on optimization, you can make use of Google's very own guide about SEO (Search Engine Optimization).

When I want to bury something - First up, you will have to work twice as hard. Dig into you social media accounts and delete photos that show your negative side. You cannot totally eradicate the negative footprints, but you want to lessen the blow.

Then afterwards, build all the positive ones. If all the recruiters can find are positive, they have not the time, nor the effort to search further.

Step 3: Prepare For Possible Interview Questions And Answers

A smart job seeker knows how important it is to either prepare for a one on one or phone interview. It may come as a surprise to you, but the hardest part of the interview preparation is not even researching about the company, it is anticipating possible questions the interviewer is bound to ask you and knowing how best to answer. Here are some of the most commonly asked questions by a majority of employers. Try to see how you would answer the following questions and find out how you would fare:

Tell me about yourself

This is the most commonly asked question in most interviews, and is probably the first thing you will hear. Be aware that this is the opportunity to introduce yourself to your interviewer. Take this time to present the most important details about yourself. Make sure that you answer this question taking into consideration how your qualifications are related to what the employer needs.

What experience do you have that makes you the best person for this job?

This is the best time to define how your previous experiences, both paid and unpaid, are tailored into the job description. Highlight your transferable skills and let your potential employer know how these skills will come in handy in the company.

What are your weaknesses?

Your interviewers will take this chance to gauge your honesty, so the best approach is to tell them about your real weaknesses in such a way that will not ruin your chances. Let your answer end in a positive note to show that you are taking measures to improve yourself. For instance, rather than saying that you find it hard speaking to a large group, you could say that you always need to prepare extensively when presenting a project to avoid silly mistakes.

Why are you interested in this position in this particular company?

This question is meant to determine what exactly caught your attention about the company in the first place. This is where your research will come into play. Keep this question in mind when you are researching in order to come up with the major reasons why you want this job.

Where do you see yourself in 5 years?

A smart employer wants to hire ambitious people who will help progress the company to the next level as they achieve their own personal goals as well. It is not necessary to have your whole future laid out, but having a clear sense of your long-term education and career goals will help a lot.

What superhero power would you like and why?

This is just one among several oddball questions interviewers like to ask. These questions have several functions. Some use them to see how interviewees would react under pressure, but the main purpose is to determine your critical thinking skills. So, the answer is not really important, but the reasoning behind it. Some people find it more effective to treat the interview like a blind date as it shows that you are genuine.

It is also fine to ask for a moment to think about the answer in order to calm your nerves, but be fun and creative when answering these oddball questions.

Why should we employ you?

While the easiest answer to this question is that you are the best candidate for this job, don't be afraid to say it, but avoid coming off as arrogant at the same time. The trick is to back your statement with the key points that distinguish you specifically. Explain this with passionate examples and remember to always tailor your answers with what you can bring to the company. Most employers save this questions until the end of the interview.

Do you have any questions?

This question is not so much about your knowledge about the company or your past experiences. This is your opportunity to interview your interviewer and illustrate your interest in the job. Avoid questions about working hours, benefits and salary, and instead concentrate on questions that will help you verify whether you want to work in that company.

The Unexpected Interview Questions... And How to Answer Them Effectively

Okay, you have learned about the most common interview questions that reviewers typically ask the applicants, but what if they do not ask those questions. What if they want to put you on the spot? In this section you will learn about the Top Unexpected Questions that interviewers would like to throw at future employees.

You have to note that these questions are logical. Meaning they should really be asked, but some employers don't want to make you feel uncomfortable. That is changing now. They would like to see how you will respond in times of pressure and unexpected "offensive" situations.

So, here are the most unexpected questions that you really should expect:

1. Why are you still unemployed up to now?

Well, this question is like a punch to the gut. It can be interpreted as something like, "Why would we hire you when others didn't?" to "Are you slacking?"

Relax. The answer to this question is really simple– just tell them that it is easy to find a job, but you don't want to settle for less. What you want to have is the RIGHT job so you eagerly pursued the company.

2. What made you leave your current job?

Employers would like to know why you left– is it because of the salary? Is it because they fired you? Is it because you cannot get along well with other employees? These are all danger topics so stray from mentioning any of them. And even if those were your reasons for leaving, don't mention them!

Instead, tell that you are looking for a change in dynamics. You want to develop more on your career and their company can provide you with the opportunity.

3. How do you view your boss?

This is a tricky question; it may seem that the recruiter wanted to know the bad sides of your previous boss, but no! He wants to know if YOU will trash talk him or not.

Remember, the one interviewing you may be your boss in the future and he wants to know if you are capable of downgrading him in front of the others. The technique here is to honestly tell the recruiter the positive points your previous boss has. If he asks you about the negative side, tell him something that is not degrading, like "He likes the office to be really quiet… so, we often whisper among each other."

4. Provide an instance when you or your works were criticized.

Another tricky question, "criticized" is a term almost always related to "negative review", but there are also positive criticisms! Make sure that the examples you will give are the times when you were positively criticized.

5. Are considering other companies as of now?

Don't panic! The interviewer is not saying that you are not accepted. He just wants to know how dedicated you are in the industry you are pursuing. So, if the position you are applying to is a Web Designer, don't tell the recruiter that you can also be a teacher because you gained units in education. That will only show that you are not serious enough to stick with the job.

6. If I talk to your boss right now, what will he tell me about you?

Again, go for the positive points, but be honest. "My boss will mention about my inclination to beat the deadlines, how I never missed one and I always submit things way before the end date. He'll also mention my ability to think out of the box, how my ideas are always unique, but doable."

7. What trends do you notice in the industry now?

You can use your research here, make it focused on what the company is trying to achieve, but make it short. The longer you state your views, the higher the chances of mistakes. Avoid figures because you might also get them wrong!

Golden Rules of Answering Job Interview Questions

These are the 5 golden rules when answering questions for a job interview. Remember this and add it to your stash of "must do's".

1. Clarify

If there are certain things in his questions that are vague, don't hesitate to ask for clarification. In fact, an intelligently constructed query will do you good. It'll tell them that you are listening and that you are interested in the question they asked.

2. Stay Honest

Never tell the recruiter things that you CANNOT do, just so he will be impressed.

3. Keep the topics neutral

If he asks you for a small talk regarding your interests, keep the topics neutral. Things like Religion, sports, and politics are red zones. He may have a completely different view on those areas that may result to the two of you "arguing".

4. Be clear

When speaking, make sure that you speak clearly, and your message does not have any other meaning aside from the one you intend to deliver.

5. Ask for a feedback

At least once, ask the recruiter if you have provided the correct information regarding his queries.

Step 4: Know The Dress Code

The kind of clothes you wear to an interview tells a lot about yourself. Therefore, it is best to choose your attire well to present yourself as the best candidate to hire. Some employers often use interview attire to test your familiarity of both the company and the industry. Here are some tips to dress for a positive effect:

*The right attire for your interview will depend on the industry, the time of the year and the geographic location.

*Take time to research about the company, its competitors and the industry on the internet to identify suitable outfits.

*If you are still not sure, you could still call the HR department of that company and inquire about the proper attire recommendation.

*When in doubt, it is always safer to show up slightly over dressed as opposed to come up looking too casual.

*If you don't have the proper outfit, visit your nearest department store and ask for help from a personal shopper.

*Make sure that your clothes are clean and well pressed.

*Avoid wearing a strong cologne or perfume

*Wear appropriate jewelry and makeup relevant to the company/job/industry.

The clothes you wear can influence your chances of landing a job. If you wore a black suit in a warm climate going for a job interview as a construction worker, the interviewer might think that you have lost your mind. Why? The clothes are not only inappropriate for the industry and advertised position, but also for the time of the year and geographic location.

Interview Attire Basics Depending on the Company

The above things discussed are the general rules, they can apply to most of the companies, but in case you want to look like you really belong, you need specific rules depending on the type of company you are applying to.

1. For reserved companies

Usually these are corporations which occupy a whole building. Their employees work while wearing suits so an applicant should follow the same protocol. Your best choice is a dark-colored suit paired with a light colored undershirt or blouse.

Women should not wear strapless tees. To help you ascertain if you are wearing the correct undershirt, remove the suit and see if it will still pass as corporate attire.

2. For casual companies

These companies are usually about technology. The employees here commonly wear casual clothes, even printed shirts and jeans, but since you still are not part of the company, being a little overdressed is your best option. This is to show that you are seriously looking to be accepted.

For men, suits aren't necessary, but still wear a decent, collared shirt and slacks. Girls can wear a semi-casual blouse with cardigan and pair it up with either slacks of black skirt.

As for the shoes, always opt for a closed, mid-heeled pair. Never show up wearing casual sandals.

Details to remember:

1. Bring either a suitcase or a purse - Go for a plain, possibly leather design.

2. Check if your nails are clean and polished with neutral color. Don't wear brightly colored nail.

3. Show your face. Avoid hairstyles that cover even just a small part of your face. Another thing is to not show up with wet hair.

4. Take note of your watch, it should also be formal, or semi-formal.

Waiting For The Interview

Step 5: Be Punctual

As a general rule of thumb, always make sure you arrive on time when called for a job interview. Most employers would agree that the best time to arrive is fifteen to twenty minutes earlier, but not sooner or later. If you are not sure how much time it takes to get to the location, you can visit the place one day prior to the meeting, taking into account the time taken from your place, and the traffic at the time of the interview. This will give a general idea of what time to get out of the house on the D-day.

Have several copies of your resume ready

This is for when they instantly opt for a panel interview. While most companies will be prepared for it (they will print multiple copies of your resumes and distribute them to the panel), there's nothing wrong with preparing your own copies. If they decided for an impromptu panel, you can hand out your copies and they will admire you for being ready. It will also indicate how serious you are to getting the job.

Do the same for your contact information and references.

Prepare some of your portfolio

If it is applicable, bringing your accomplishments with you will also help them ascertain whether you are fit for the job or not.

What To Do

Stay Calm

The fifteen minutes before that job interview can be traumatic, to say the least. Most job seekers are not sure what to do with this time. However, the best advice at this point is to look in a mirror, breathe deeply and try to stay calm. When you are stressed out, your body releases stress hormones such as epinephrine and cortisol. When this happens, depending on the level of your stress, your ability to think clearly can be vastly affected. This is why it is important that you remain cool, calm and collected in the few minutes leading to the interview.

Be Friendly To Everyone

As soon as you walk into the waiting room of the company in question, remember to be nice to the security guards, receptionist and anyone who greets you. Chances are the person might be reporting back to the employer or hiring manager on how you conducted yourself.

Determine What You Want To Be Remembered For

This could be your project management skills, your communication skills or your knowledge. Being keen on a few things that will make you more likeable and memorable is a smart way to embrace the interview.

Don't Rehearse Here

This is not the time to rehearse or over prepare for responses as this can make your conversation appear scripted and unauthentic. While it is necessary to know your details, it is important to keep in mind that the interview is more like a conversation. Trust in your knowledge and that the interview will flow on its own.

Breathe

This is a great tip to help you keep calm. Just take huge breaths, focusing on each breath and count until you reach ten to calm your nerves. This is one of the most recognized and proven relaxation techniques.

Focus on your Posture

When you are waiting to be called in the interview room, sit up straight and don't slouch. This will make you appear more poised and confident.

Turn Your Phone Off (Not On Vibrate)

No matter how tempted you are, make sure that your phone is turned off as soon as you arrive at the interview location. In addition, avoid checking your email, voicemail or your social media accounts. You may read or hear something that might get you distracted or get you worked up, which is one of the worst things that can happen at that time.

Review Your Notes Briefly

By now, you should be done with all the preparation, research and rehearsals, but if you made a few notes during these processes, you can look at them briefly.

Look In The Mirror

Find a nearby clothing store or restroom and check yourself in the mirror. While you may have left your house looking dazzling, anything can happen on the way and you end up in the waiting room unkempt. Use this time to wash your hands and ascertain that your palms are dry and your fingernails are clean.

Think Happy Thoughts

You may have heard this a thousand times before, but thinking pleasant thoughts that make you feel good and smile can go a long way in putting you in the right state of mind as you enter the interview room.

STEP 6: Be Courteous

Even if you have an exceptional CV and the hiring manager cannot wait to meet you, there is still a lot to do before you are hired. The best way to clear the huddles to the job offer is to demonstrate a positive and friendly attitude throughout the interview process. This applies at all stages of the interview: as soon as you arrive, when waiting, and after the interview. How you behave can tell a lot about the kind of person you really are. If the interviewer or administrative assistant offers you something to drink, maintain a friendly smile and either decline or accept graciously. Chances are this will trigger positive feelings from the person issuing the hospitality. Be nice to everyone you meet at the location of the interview. Smile and use a friendly tone to make a positive impression. In addition, pay attention to your body language. Your body language is a powerful indicator of your feelings at that particular moment, and it is an important tool of demonstrating friendliness. Here are a few tips to boost your etiquette:

Use Ms or Mr when addressing your interviewers

Have you ever noticed that most people prefer to be called by their first name? When last did you hear someone instruct you to refer to him or her with his or her last name? The main reason for this is that using the last name when addressing someone is a show of respect. In a world where little of this is going around, you are more likely to stand out from the crowd. NB: throughout your interview, the interviewer will be trying to assess how easy it will be to manage and work with you. As much as employers are looking for leaders and self starters, sometimes they need someone who can do his/her job and act like a soldier.

Look People In The Eye

As a point of emphasis, body language is very important when it comes to displaying appropriate interview etiquette. Studies have shown that about 80 percent of our conversations are non verbal. One good way to build trust and connect with people is to look them in the eyes. This also applies when you find yourself in a group interview. Most people tend to show nervousness when under pressure, lack confidence and don't usually smile. Something as simple as a friendly smile can make the world of difference in showcasing leadership and confidence, even if you are a nervous wreck.

Firm Handshake

If you have made it this far, chances are you are going to greet your interviewer by hand. Be prepared for this. Make sure that your palms are not sweaty. A handshake is another non verbal way of connecting with people. While it may seem ludicrous to be judged by a limp handshake, it happens all the time. However, be cautious with this advice. Make sure your handshake is not too firm, especially if you are a man shaking a woman's hand. You don't want to break your interviewer's bones on your first day!

Let the interviewer lead the interview

If your interviewer appears to be somehow laid back or soft spoken, you may feel the urge to get things moving by trying to take back some control. Before you know it, you are rambling. Overcome this temptation and let the hiring manager run the show. If you experience moments of silence, just embrace the silence. If you are adequately prepared for the interview, then you have nothing to worry about. Talking too much is one of the most common mistakes people get wrong during interviews.

Avoid Interrupting

Some people have a bad habit of interrupting someone else when speaking. This very annoying habit shows lack of courtesy. Let the person interviewing you finish making their point and then add to the conversation or respond to their question.

Sit Up And Lean Slightly Forward

Even if you have the excellent qualifications, you stand a very big chance of being rejected just for being too laid back in the interview, I mean literally. This is one of the most common reasons older candidates are often prejudged as lacking in ambition and drive. However, you also need to be on your guard even if you are a younger job seeker to avoid coming out too relaxed or casual.

Chase The Job Even If The Interview Is Going Badly

Even if the interview seems to be taking the opposite train as opposed to your plans and you desperately wish you were out of there, it is advisable to stay professional and continue with your interview to the best of your abilities. Always remember that you are in control because you can always turn down the offer or withdraw from the process. As a general rule of thumb, always make it a point to wait for all the facts before you can make a final judgment about a company or an individual.

Watch Yourself Until You Get Out Of The Interview Location

Some hiring managers have the tendency to watch candidates as they exit the building through their office window. People can do some pretty astonishing things like lighting up a cigarette, spitting, talking on their cell phones for 30 minutes, arranging themselves while leaning on their cars, and other unbelievable things. The best advice is to stay in a professional mode, at least until you get out of sight.

The Body Language Red Flags

During the interview consider the following body language red flags. Avoid them because they send out meanings that you don't want to deliver in an interview. Keep in mind that a job interview is a formal communication. You cannot afford to break your chance just because you have a bad habit you could not get rid of.

Most companies are objective in their hiring process, but you have to be honest. The recruiter is bound to make a judgment based on what he sees, and if even he sees something he does not like, he may automatically shred your application.

These are the Body Language Pitfalls you must avoid:

Pointing

During the interview, the recruiter sets a distance between him and the applicant. This is to keep things professional. Although not obviously, pointing your finger at the person you are talking to breaks that space. The act in itself is accusatory and blaming, so avoid doing this during the interview.

Crossing the arms over the chest

Crossing your arms over your chest is a very defensive gesture. It's as if you do not want the interviewer to know anything about you, which cannot be because the purpose of the interview is to let them know how you can contribute to their company. On top of that, this gesture will make the recruiter feel like you are overriding his authority, as if whatever you say is right and you do not care what he thinks about it.

Fidgeting

Fidgeting is a very distracting body language and it delivers the message that you are not confident. Examples of fidgeting are nail biting, wringing your hands, continuously tapping your feet, and playing with the seams of your suit.

When you are talking, the goal is to make the interviewer see your point. He won't be able to concentrate if you are fidgeting will catch his attention.

Nodding too much

Nodding too much is a common mistake among applicants. In their desire to let the interviewer know that they are listening and that they understand, they always nod. The problem here is it distracts the interviewer and instead of thinking that you indeed comprehend what he is telling you, he will think of the opposite: you don't really understand that's why you keep on nodding!

So nod once or twice and focus.

Hands behind the back or inside the pockets

Like crossing the arms, hands in the pocket or at your back means that you are unwilling to be approached. Most applicants do this to prevent themselves from fidgeting; but still, this is a major body language red flag. The interviewer will feel like you are holding back and your lack of comfort will dominate the whole interview.

Staring

Because you do not want to break the eye contact, you opt for staring too much! Don't do that, for one thing, that's a creepy gesture and second, it will look like you are the one who is scrutinizing the interviewer. Just be natural and don't forget to blink.

Mismatched facial expression

Sometimes, what your voice implies seem different from what your expression shows. Doing this (even though most of the time it is unintentional) will make the recruiter think that you are pretentious. Don't be too caught up on the rule that you have to smile. If what you are talking about is a serious discussion, opt for a serious expression and soften it if the conversation shifts to a more pleasant track.

The Tone of Your Confidence

Now that you are equipped with the right and wrong gestures, it's time to increase the level of your confidence by letting it show in your voice. In this section we will discuss about the proper ways of making you sound confidence without being rude.

1. Have a powerful pause

After the interviewer fires a question, ponder about it first for a few seconds before answering. The common mistake applicant makes is answering right away with thinking their answer's train of thought. Although it will feel like 5 seconds is a very long time to pause, the interviewer takes it positively because it will show that you "organize" things first in your head before answering.

2. Getting read of monotony

While talking, be natural. Don't let your nervousness make your answer monotonous. Another thing to avoid is increasing the tone of your voice in the end of a statement, Doing that can change the nature of your message from a well-stated fact, to an unsure question.

3. Never blabber

Avoid filler words like "Uhm..." and "Ah..." These words imply the recruiter of your uncertainty.

4. The positive tone

Positive tone reflects your confidence by making your words clear; you tone calm, and you choice of words appropriate.

5. A fact is a fact

Don't use weak phrases like "I think..." and "I believe..." for statements that you are actually sure of! For example, if the interviewer asks you if you know how to design a website, don't answer with "I think I know how to design a website", when in you know deep down that you do.

What to do if you are stumped in an interview?

Although you have exerted a great deal of effort for the job interview, there are instances when the interviewer is a really tough person. It's as if his goal is to get you rejected. Or if not that, may be all the techniques you have read about flew out of the window because of fear and anxiety.

If you do not know how and what to respond to a certain query, what will you do? Here are some great tips for you:

1. Keep calm

Being unable to answer a question is a huge stressor, so you have to keep it cool. Once the symptoms of stress show, thinking clearly will become even more difficult. So take a deep breath and reassure yourself that unexpected things really happen.

And remember to clarify... you know the answer, it's just that you got the question wrong.

2. "I don't know." Is an empty expression

Even though you really don't know what to make of the question, don's immediately say you don't know. These words are empty. It means that in the times when you are cornered and restricted, you are unable to find a way to resolve a problem.

Surely, although not the exact answer, you have an idea that is closely related to the topic. So inform him of the things that you know. NEVER make things up just so you can cover up your lack of knowledge.

Another good alternative is to tell the recruiter your ways of finding out the answer. This will give them the message that you are resourceful, sure, you don't know the answer now but it does not mean you will not know the answer forever.

3. But still be honest…

If the question is an "exam" type, or those queries that have exact answers (numbers, places, names of people) and you really don't know what to tell the interviewer, then be honest and admit it. But still, avoid saying I don't know. Instead of that expression why not consider this one: I still have no come across that fact, I'll be sure to read about that later. May be I can e-mail you the answer?

When the conversation drives toward the salary…

Be prepared, the employer or the recruiter will definitely ask you about your salary expectations. If they give you more than you are expecting, congratulations! But what if you really like the job, but the salary is to meager for your liking?

Is there a chance that you can negotiate for it? There is!

Follow these tips when negotiating about the salary:

1. Don't bring it up

For one, the talk about the salary will most likely surface even without you initiating the topic. If you do, you will look like you are just there for the money and not for the career. The only time you will have to bring up the topic about the salary is when they make you sign papers right away even when they did not mention what the pay will be. If that situation arises, inquire about the money on the line— it is your right.

2. Have a firm resolve

Before walking inside the building, have a firm resolve about the salary you will be accepting. Don't settle for a stiff figure, have a range instead. Salary negotiation is accepted, remember this, if you are really fit for the job, the company needs you as much as you need them, so they will be willing to give you the salary you feel you deserve.

The problem happens when you do not know what your salary should be, so before the interview, have the range ready.

3. What you are worth– nothing below that

Research on the internet about the salary range applicable to you. Make sure that the data will be coming from people whose credentials are almost the same as yours. And of course, also consider your company, review the job requirements, and the possible work if you are hired. It's much better if you know someone from inside the company whose position is the same as the one you are applying for, but of course don't demand that they tell you.

During the interview, calmly talk about it to the recruiter. Make your points clear and convincing.

4. What about the company?

This is very important, from the start, if you know that the company is having financial issues, don't negotiate too much. However, if you know deep down that they are doing so well, and they can afford to give you the salary you deserve, you have to negotiate. Don't get stuck in a job where you know you should be earning more, you will only feel deprived and your performance will be affected.

5. Get the support of the recruiter

Another point you have to understand is this: when the companies hire people to screen applicants, they do not have the final say on your salary. What you can do is sell yourself to them so that they will support your salary package. While you are in the interview room, don't frown on the recruiter just because he or she is unable to satisfy your demands, it really just not his place. Be good to him or her because once the interview is over, he will "talk" to the boss to make your negotiations! If you rum him off the wrong way, he may not even make the effort!

Areas you can negotiate about:

Perks - The companies offer perks to their employees. It can be in any form, like night differential, bonuses, signing initiatives, and vacation days. Some of them are easier to negotiate while the others will be hard. So, gauge it. What do you want to achieve? What do you value more? If you are in great need for money, a signing bonus should be your top priory, likewise if you love having vacations, concentrate on that.

The salary grade - If the company's rules for promotions are too stiff, you might want to negotiate about the salary grade instead. That way, even if you are not promoted, you will still be getting the pay you deserve.

The duration - If it is impossible for the pay grade to be increased, at least negotiate about the duration it will take for you to have higher salary. For example, it typically takes one year before a higher rate is achieved; negotiate it to be 6 months.

Things you can say to have a successful negotiation:

"What is the salary range of your employees who have the same position as the one I am applying for?"

This is a good starting question when the talk about salary is initiated. The recruiter will most likely answer it because you have the right to know about the pay grade. It will give the edge to calculate whether the salary they have is within the range you have in mind.

"I want to know more about the job, what it entails, who I will be answering to…"

This is a very good statement when the recruiter is insisting that you give a definite figure for your salary expectation. It will give you the idea if the job is too much, or it is light.

"Is the figure flexible?"

Just remember to be calm and collected when asking this question. If you feel like the grade they have provided you is better that your expectation, don't prod anymore, but if you think the grade is too low for the job, start negotiating with this question. Whether the recruiter answers Yes or No, at least you will be prepared.

"That's disappointing…"

Believe it or not, this is a very acceptable statement. If you are confident of your skills and credentials, you have every right to be disappointed if the salary grade is too low. Again, they need you as much as you need them, and if you are really good, may be they need you more. So, follow it up with "What can we do to figure it out?"

"Will that be in my contract?"

If you manage to negotiate the salary that you want, make sure that it is put to writing. Just because the recruiter verbally agreed to increase your grade doesn't mean it is final. Wait for it to be put in paper before taking a deep breath.

"Let us review it again after 3 months..."

If you feel that the reason behind the refusal to increase your salary grade is because they seem to not trust your skills, offer to have probation of 3 months. But be sure to also put it in writing! This is a very fair negotiation and most of the time, it works!

Remember this: Negotiations about salary grade is acceptable. It will not make you look like you're only it for the money. If you do not negotiate, then the answer is automatically no. You will be imprisoned with a job that should be paying you more, but isn't.

How to Handle Harassment and Illegal Questions during the Interview

Although it does not happen often, harassment during an interview is not unheard of. This is especially true for female applicants being interviewed by male recruiters; however, it can also happen to men.

From asking illegal questions to being hit on and sexually harassed, here are some of the guidelines on how to come out of the interview room with your dignity intact, and your job opportunity still safe.

You only have to keep in mind that the decision is still yours, and you have to follow what your gut tells you. The following are just guidelines and your affinity to abide by them depends on several factors like the degree of harassment (or is it really harassment) and how much do you need or want the job.

In this section we will discuss the possible acts you can do, as well as the advantage and disadvantage of that act. That way, you will have the final say– are you going to pursue the interview, or walk away and never contact that company again?

Walk away politely –

Walking away politely means you will end the interview immediately. The logic behind this is who wants to be a part of a company where the HR can harass the applicant? The downside of this decision is this: you may never get the job in that corporation. So, think carefully about the following:

Are you really harassed? If the recruiter seems like he is hitting on you, was the approach offending? Or was he just trying to appease your nervousness? If you weren't really uncomfortable in his choice of words, go on with the interview.

However, if the recruiter touches you in such a way that made you uncomfortable, or worse if he asked you for a date or sex in exchange of the job, you should draw the line. Your decision to walk away is justified. The next step is to report the problem to the other authorities in the company.

Continue with the interview–

Should you decide to continue with the job interview regardless of the degree of harassment, and you managed to pass it, you should attend the second interview and hope that the next recruiter is accommodating of your complaint. He or she may tact away your issue and promise to bring it to the authority using due process and then go on with the interview. He may also refuse to believe you because you are "still" an applicant and they may question your credibility.

Accepting the job offer–

In case you get through everything and they finally offer you the job, don't forget to mention the incident to your boss. Should he refuse to believe you and dismiss your complaint, why would you bother working under him? You might want to decline the job offer.

The only downside is this: you will be initiating trouble– sure you were not the one who started it, but others might already see you as the trouble maker.

You SHOULD take action

If harassment happened, you should always take action, especially if you really felt violated by the interviewer's act. Tell the interviewer that you feel uncomfortable and that it is the interview and the career that you are focused on. REFUSE any form of harassment. For one, remember that this is an interview; the recruiter might just be "testing" you, and is just waiting for your next move. This is highly unlikely, but you should never dismiss the possibility that all is a farce. You have to refuse.

On top of that, if you don't take action, only the bad will happen. You might get the job but you have to continuously be reminded that you had it by submitting to the recruiter's illegal demands, he may even keep you on the leash because of that and your job will be hellish.

Handling the Illegal Questions

Unbeknownst to many, there are illegal questions that an interviewer should never ask– what they are and how to answer them will be discussed here. The idea is there should not be any form of discrimination– you should be judge on your skills and your experiences, not by your age, religion, color, and origin.

Any question that relates to a person's age should be off limits -

Yes, you may not know it, but it is illegal for a recruiter to ask a question that will reveal your age. Consider this– you are already in an interview room, so it is a given that they have already accepted some of your credentials, diploma and the like. Why is there a need for the recruiter to know your age? It opens the possibility of discrimination.

A tricky example is this: "What was the year when you graduated in high school?" or "When is your birthday?"

If he asks how long are you working for a specific industry, that's acceptable.

"Are you a social drinker?"

An employer or a recruiter should never ask you about your drinking habits. The logic here is that you might be an alcoholic before, but you have recovered and now you are living a productive life. It's discriminatory to judge you with your past conditions. This fact is legally stated. The Americans with Disabilities Act dictates that a recovering alcoholic should never reveal his condition before having a job.

"How much debt do you have?"

The recruiter doesn't have the right to ask you about any outstanding debt, or your credit card history unless this information will hoper your skills in performing the tasks assigned in the position you are applying for. This includes questions that indirectly ask about the properties you own.

"Are you a native English speaker?"

It is highly unlawful to judge a person by the main language that he uses in speaking. He has the right to know how fluent you speak in a given language because that may directly affect your capability to perform certain functions, but there never should be an issue about the first and the main language that you use.

"What country are you from?"

This is a very innocent question, especially if you have an accent that is very noticeable, but remember that it is still an illegal question. Answering this will reveal your nationality, a factor that will not play any role in your performance. Instead, employers can ask if you have the authority to work on certain countries.

"How many children do you have?"

Asking if you have children is already illegal, what more if the recruiter will ask you how many do you have? Be weary of this because employers really, really take into consideration if you have a family to attend to. They think that just because you have children, you won't be able to perform your job to the best of your ability– this is a form of discrimination.

He also should not ask you if you are planning to have a baby in the foreseeable future. Their questions should be geared towards the amount of time you could dedicate for the position you are applying for. Great examples of those questions are: "How much time can you allocate for this job?" and "Are there any obligations that you think will interfere with your performance?"

"What religious practices do you perform and when?"

Since the question reveals your religion, it is illegal. The recruiter may just want to know the times of the year which you are available for work, so this question should have been constructed properly like– "Will you be able to work on Sundays?"

As a general rule, it is illegal for the recruiter to ask you questions that will reveal the following:

- Age
- Sexual orientation
- Race
- National origin
- Birthplace
- Color
- Disability
- Marital status

How to handle illegal questions:

When faced with illegal questions, there are several ways by which you can respond. Keep in mind that some recruiters may not really wish to be discriminative, the questions are just so innocent-sounding that it slips their mind that they are illegal to ask. However, they are still unlawful so you have the right to decline answering them.

Use the following guidelines in dodging the illegal questions while still maintaining an air of professionalism:

1. Answer the questions - If it does not make you uncomfortable and the recruiter seems to be genuinely curious, you may opt to answer the question. For example, the hiring manager may be a little curious about your age because you look rather young for the position you are applying for.

2. Answer the purpose of the question - It may be that the reason why the recruiter is asking about your citizenship is because he wants to know if you are authorized to work in the area. So, answer the intent of the question instead of revealing your citizenship. The same for the first language, he just might want to know if you have competent English speaking skills, so politely tell him that you are fluent in both written and spoken English, no need to reveal your first language.

3. Refuse to answer the question - you can do this is two steps, first if the conversation just went out of the way because the both of you became comfortable, swiftly change the topic and bring it back to the interview process. If the recruiter insists on questioning you illegally, calmly tell him that you are not comfortable and that you wish to move on to the next set of questions.

After The Interview

Step 7: Follow Up

While you don't want to come out as too arrogant or too annoying, you don't want your silence to be misinterpreted as indifference. As such, it is always wise to follow up to find out the current state of affairs. There are several ways you can do this, including:

Sending A Thank You Note

This should be done as soon as the interview is through, preferably on your way out using your smart phone. If this is not possible, you could still send the email in the evening or when you get home. This will show the interviewer that you are organized and enthusiastic and is a great way to ensure that they will not forget you. Include your phone number, full name, email address and the mailing address on the thank you note. If you wait too long before sending that thank you note, you may appear disinterested in the job and another candidate can beat you to the race. Also, if there was someone who helped you set up the interview, do not forget to send them a thank you note as well. While some people prefer handwritten notes, some interviewers may perceive this as being unprofessional as it is somewhat outdated. Therefore, the best approach here is to send an email.

Make Notes On The Interview

Write down the notes about the interview as soon as possible as these may come in handy during a second interview. You can use these to recall the topics of conversation and any personality traits and qualifications that your interviewer emphasized on as being relevant for this position. This is a great way to give you an idea of where you went wrong if you are not called for a second interview. On the other hand, you can use these notes to modify your responses in case of a second interview. In addition, the notes can also help you with your follow up thank you note as you refer to more specific points of the interview. This will show that you were really paying close attention to what the interviewer was saying.

Inquire To Connect On Linkedin

It is absolutely appropriate to ask your interviewer to connect with you on LinkedIn, if you do it right. On one hand, you don't want to come off looking over confident about getting the job, and on the other hand, you don't want your motives to appear completely selfish. The best approach is to send a small message explaining who you are while stating a few points from the interview before you ask to connect on LinkedIn. For example, if you are applying for a position in the fashion industry, and the subject of Paris Fashion Week was raised during the interview, you can cite an interesting article about a particular fashion trend or designer that you found on the internet and ask if it is okay to share it with them. On the other hand, if you had a casual conversation with your interviewer and something came up about a certain upcoming music or even restaurant, you can ask to share a link with additional details. The trick is to make it worthwhile or interesting for them as you request to connect on LinkedIn; let it not look like a completely self serving move.

Most Common Causes of Rejection

The causes of rejection can be divided into two categories, The first one is the factors that you cannot control, and the second one are the factors you had control of but did not manage to make the best out of the effort.

Factors that you have no control of are the following:

They opt to hire internally

This is when the company chose a candidate who is already working in the company. You should not feel bad about it because competing with that candidate is really tough. He already knows the twists and turns of the company so the higher ups are really more likely to choose him.

The HR just don't like you

You have to be honest with yourself, no matter how objective the company is when it comes to the hiring process, personal opinion of the recruiter still counts. You have done everything, but your chemistry with the recruiters really didn't seem to work. Not that the recruiter has something against you, but for some mysterious reason he sees you as someone who is not fit for the job.

Job revision and cancellation

Yes, it is possible. Even though the company has taken all the effort to post the job and interview candidates, there is still chance that he job will be cancelled or the description will be revised, again you must not feel bad about it.

The factors that you can control are the following:

Lack of preparation

If you did not prepare for the interview, get ready to be rejected. The fact that you lack preparation is a testament of how you do not really like the job. The recruiter will feel like you just wasted their time–lack of preparation includes being late, knowing nothing about the company, inappropriate outfit, and not being able to answer their queries confidently.

Lack of energy

Again, the employers are looking for spontaneity; they want to see desire and energy. If you will come in the interview room and look very bored, they will feel offended and your resume will go straight to the shredder.

Lack of questions

Each interview will give you this one liner at the very end: "Do you have any questions?" Never say "None!" You must have at least one question; otherwise they will think that you just wanted to get over the interview process. Before going to your interview prepare at least three intelligent questions and when the one liner pops up, fire one of them.

Tash talking

Trash talking your previous company will not make the company you are applying for feel good. In fact, this will make them worry in case they hire you. When you trash talk your previous employer, it shows that you are not leaving them in good terms. Why would they hire someone who did not get along well with others? They will think that when the time comes that you resign from them; you will also down talk them.

You are not in it for the long haul

You have to understand that employers will invest time and money to you. Once you are hired, they will train you, you will have the first hand knowledge about the company. If they get the idea that you will only be with them for a few months, what's the point of hiring you? They will even think of you as a job hopper! The technique is to have the mindset that you will stay with them for years.

Your references did not vouch for you

Your references are a big part of judging. Keep in mind that the company know nothing about you, they will have to inquire someone about how you perform. They may give you the benefit of the doubt if only one of your references trashed talk you, but if all three of them say the same thing, then your name will be crossed out immediately.

The points are these:

You did not get along with them

You are not doing your job properly

And you have no one who will vouch for you (if you have you should have included their names!)

You did not sell your success

Having the experience is not enough; you have to market your success. So instead of just mentioning your previous job description, highlight all your successes. Bring your portfolio; tell them stories for when a project became successful because of you.

Overconfidence

Although you want to showcase your confidence, being overly confident will only get you in trouble. As mentioned, you have to let them lead the interview process. When they feel like you are interviewing them too (you really should but you should never be obvious!), they will mistake that as an act of being cocky. Don't ask questions unless they have invited you to, and watch the tone of your voice!

Bad online reputation

And lastly, having a bad online rep can lead to rejection. So take into consideration the step by step guide we have provided in the book for building a positive online presence.

Several Days Afterwards

Step 8: Forward A More Formal Thank You Note

You can do this either through a typed letter or via email, depending on the nature of the company you are applying to. A tech company or a social media related company might appreciate the efficiency and simplicity of an email, while an old fashioned company would appreciate a letter. Whatever method you decide to use, the point here is to remind the interviewer that you are a strong candidate and why you are specially qualified for the position. If a group of people interviewed you, send each one of them a separate letter. Unless you were instructed to refer to your interviewers with their first name, address them in a formal manner in the greeting and salutation. After you have thanked the interviewer for the interview opportunity, affirm your interest in the job and reemphasize your role as an asset to the company. Include any information that they may be interested in or the company could use. This is a smart move to make your interviewer remember you since most people only follow up after a job interview with their own information. Make sure you close the letter with "yours sincerely" and don't forget to check for grammar mistakes.

Step 9: Wait And Then Follow Up With A Single Phone Call Or Email

If the period your interviewer specified to reach a decision has passed, this is the right time to follow up about their decision through a phone call or email. However, just keep it cool and brief. If you prefer calling, make sure the location from where you are making the call is free of distractions and noise. In addition, find a good time to call; not early in the morning, right after lunch or at the end of the day. This way, you increase your chances of reaching the interviewer and speaking to them. Be as brief and polite as possible while you are on the phone. Keep in mind that the hiring manager could be stressed out with one hundred things on his/her mind apart from your job application. Unless you are specifically told to call, avoid calling a second time. If you are contacted about a job offer or a second interview, respond promptly. It is unprofessional to make them wait for your response, and it may make you look unenthusiastic about the job. Don't worry about coming off as too eager; the company probably wants candidates who are elated by the idea of working for them. Use the same method they used to contact you when replying. If they used an email, send an email, if they called, call them back immediately. On the other hand, make sure you thank the interviewer even if you don't get the job but for their time. Control your disappointment or anger and accept the fact there were probably countless other candidates who were over qualified and take it as a learning experience. Regardless of the method the interviewer used to contact you, remember to send a follow up message thanking them for their time and giving you an opportunity to interview with the company. If you can, ask your interviewer if they would be willing to share where you went wrong and how you can improve in the future. Chances are they might decline, but if they play a long, you could gain some credible insights into what exactly they were looking for and what you lacked. Don't beat yourself too much about it; take the suggestions as constructive criticism. You should always execute this step via email or through a letter, and not a phone call. Calling someone to ask them how you fell short of the interview or why you didn't get the job can put them in an uncomfortable position and seal your fate out of the company in case of any future open positions.

What Not To Do After The Interview

Don't harass the company

Some of the things people do after a job interview are simply out of this world and could not only ruin your chances of getting the job, but it could also close several doors for you in the future. Think about it. Imagine screwing up so badly in one interview, get employed in a competitor company, and then the two merge and you are forced to report to the same director you harassed several months ago. Being over zealous and overwhelming the company with countless phone calls and emails is the worst idea that could set you back to the job hunting stage you were once in. Use the three strike rule: a single thank you note, an extended thank you letter, and short follow up email to determine whether a decision has been made. If none of these mediums yield any response, it is always advisable to quit while you are ahead of yourself and start looking for another position. Whatever you do, avoid filling your hiring manager's inbox with countless emails or leaving long messages on their voicemail because this will definitely not do you any good.

Unless You Are Invited, Do Not Go To The Company In Person

This is a very unprofessional move to make and it puts pressure on the interviewer to talk with you, even though it may be an inconvenience time for them. It also makes it very awkward if you did not get the job and they have to tell you in person. In both cases, this is a very bad reflection and you should always avoid it at all costs, even when delivering thank you notes, just don't do it.

Don't Avoid The Follow Up Phone Call Or Letter

Some people wrongfully think that they should simply wait for the company to make a decision rather than bothering the interviewer. This tactic is not correct. Several companies deliberately wait to see who will follow up professionally after the interview before hiring. As long as you remain conservative and don't over do it, following up is a strategic and positive move that may be instrumental in landing you a job with the company.

Conclusion

Thank you again for downloading this book!

I hope this book has helped you know what you can do and what you avoid in order to ace that interview. Now you can be sure that with the tips you have learnt here, you will never fail to pass an interview again.

Finally, if you enjoyed this book, please share your thoughts and post a review on Amazon.

Thank you and good luck!

Bonus Video: What to Say In Interview

It's always good to get a visual demonstration to see what we are explaining this book. Here is a great bonus video just to give you an advantage on others that are applying for your job.

Bonus Video:
https://www.youtube.com/watch?v=hR3NrGV0JlI

www.ingramcontent.com/pod-product-compliance
Lightning Source LLC
Chambersburg PA
CBHW071759170526
45167CB00003B/1101